Congratulations, First-Time Flyer!

By
Barbara Lynn Freedman

Illustrations by
Claudia Pimentel

This book is dedicated to my mom, Joan Solomon, and to the memory of my dad, Irving Freedman. Each of them taught me so many things about life, but mainly that the the sky is not the limit — just the beginning.

- B.L.F.

For Mami and Papi, who made me a first-time flyer before I could walk, and have kept me flying ever since.

- C.P.

Today is the day you take your first flight

You may not be nervous but yet, you just might!

And arrive at the airport

With time to spare

The lines may be long and you may have to wait

But you'll soon be checked in, on your way to the gate

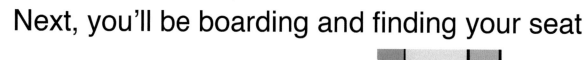

Next, you'll be boarding and finding your seat

You can listen to music or catch a few Z's

The ride may be smooth or just a bit bumpy

To help keep you safe and to serve you with smiles!

Up front in the flight deck are not one, but two

They work the computers that keep you in flight.

CERTIFICATE OF FIRST-TIME FLIGHT

FLYER'S NAME _____

DATE _____

TO/FROM (airport/city) _____

AIRLINE (flight#) _____

AUTOGRAPHS _____

Congratulations, First-Time Flyer!

www.flywithskygrrl.com

Barbara Lynn Freedman, aka "Skygrrl," calls Grand Rapids, Michigan her forever hometown. Her love of aviation and the West Michigan area inspired the moniker Skygrrl, in honor of the Gerald R. Ford International Airport, (GRR). Barbara Lynn is a flight attendant, writer and proud mom of adult children Mollie, Mitchell and Mark. When she isn't flying the fabulous skies, she can be found on the tennis courts, running trail, or leading group exercise classes. Her program, "LET'S GO FLYING!", has her visiting schools and organizations to share her love of flying and reading, and to encourage youngsters with her message: "Make All Your Dreams Take Flight!"™

Claudia Pimentel is a Grand Rapids based illustrator, cartoonist and story-maker, specializing in children's book illustration, character design, cartoon and comics works and various methods of story-telling and pancake flipping. She adores both the extremes of super-cute and graphic-cool, the vintage and the modern, and always the holy realism of the natural world. When not drawing, she enjoys singing with her daughter, playing vintage video games, cooking with leeks and hanging out with her family. Hailing from Peru, she has enjoyed flying and travel with her family since she was very small. Her favorite cities in the world are Kagoshima (Japan) Cuzco (Peru) and Grand Rapids (Michigan, USA).